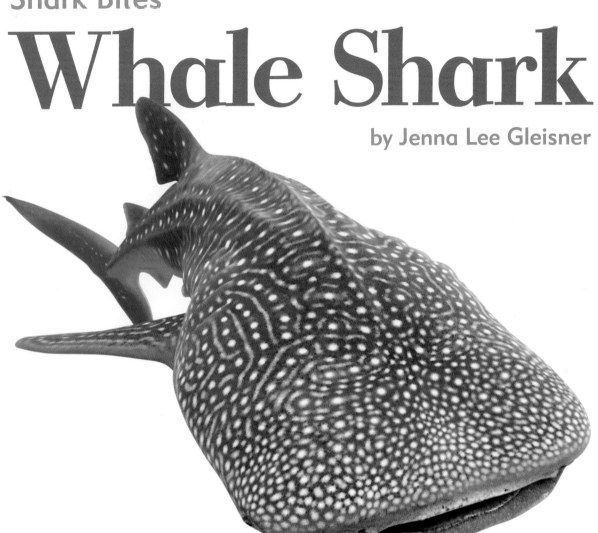

Shark Bites

Whale Shark

by Jenna Lee Gleisner

Ideas for Parents and Teachers

Bullfrog Books let children practice reading informational text at the earliest reading levels. Repetition, familiar words, and photo labels support early readers.

Before Reading

- Discuss the cover photo. What does it tell them?
- Look at the picture glossary together. Read and discuss the words.

Read the Book

- "Walk" through the book and look at the photos. Let the child ask questions. Point out the photo labels.
- Read the book to the child, or have him or her read independently.

After Reading

- Prompt the child to think more. Ask: Whale sharks earned their name because of their large size. Have you ever seen a whale or shark?

Bullfrog Books are published by Jump!
5357 Penn Avenue South
Minneapolis, MN 55419
www.jumplibrary.com

Library of Congress Cataloging-in-Publication Data

Names: Gleisner, Jenna Lee, author.
Title: Whale shark / by Jenna Lee Gleisner.
Description: Minneapolis, MN : Jump!, Inc., [2020]
Series: Shark bites
Audience: Ages 5-8. | Audience: K to grade 3.
Includes bibliographical references and index.
Identifiers: LCCN 2019001202 (print)
LCCN 2019004689 (ebook)
ISBN 9781641289702 (ebook)
ISBN 9781641289696 (hardcover : alk. paper)
Subjects: LCSH: Whale shark—Juvenile literature.
Classification: LCC QL638.95.R4 (ebook)
LCC QL638.95.R4 G54 2020 (print) | DDC 597.3—dc23
LC record available at https://lccn.loc.gov/2019001202

Editors: Susanne Bushman and Jenna Trnka
Design: Shoreline Publishing Group

Photo Credits: Crisod/iStock, cover; Krzysztof Odziomek/Dreamstime, 1, 24; Chainarong Phrammanee/Shutterstock, 3; Krzysztof Odziomek/Shutterstock, 4; Indian Ocean Imagery/iStock, 5; Helmut Cornell/Alamy, 6–7; Nature Picture Library/Alamy, 8, 20–21; Divepic/iStock, 9; Mlhtlander/iStock, 10–11, 23tr; Rich Carey/Shutterstock, 12–13, 23br; Reinhard Dirscherl/Alamy, 14–15; Helmut Cornell/Alamy, 16, 23tl; Tarpan/Dreamstime, 17; Max Topichi/iStock, 18–19; Richard Whitcombe/Shutterstock, 22; Choksawatdikom/Shutterstock, 23bl.

Printed in the United States of America at Corporate Graphics in North Mankato, Minnesota.

Table of Contents

Gentle Giant

It is huge!

It has spots.

It is a whale shark!

It is the
largest fish.

How big is it?

Up to 40 feet
(12 meters) long!

Wow!

Its body is flat.

It has a white belly.

It lives in warm waters.

It migrates in spring.

Where does it go?

Australia.

reef

Why?

To eat near this reef.

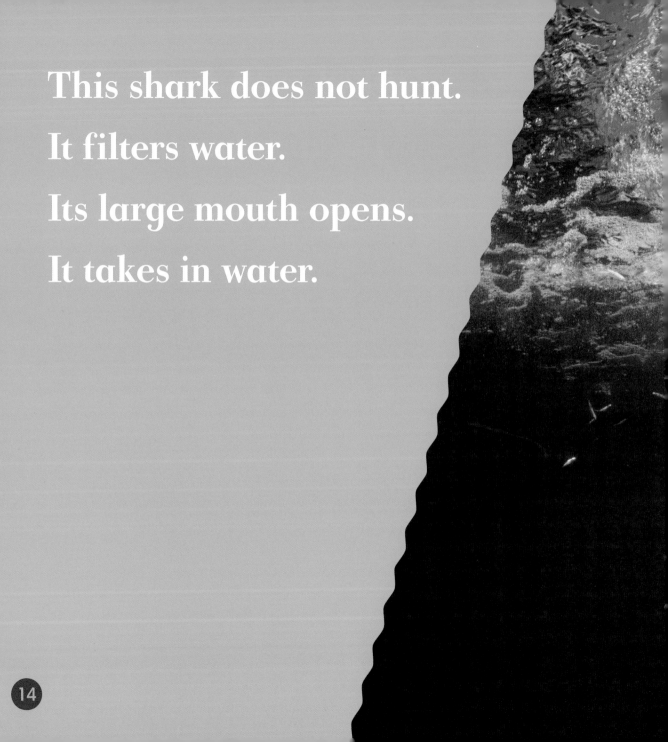

This shark does not hunt.
It filters water.
Its large mouth opens.
It takes in water.

14

Gills catch food.

gill

krill

Plankton. And krill.

Yum!

It is gentle.

It does not
mind divers.

Cool!

It can live
a long time.

How long?

Up to 70 years!

Would you like
to see one?

Parts of a Whale Shark

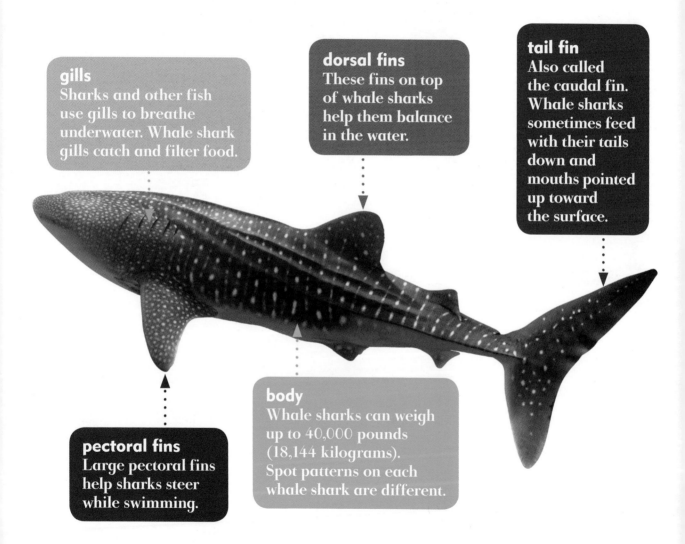

gills
Sharks and other fish use gills to breathe underwater. Whale shark gills catch and filter food.

dorsal fins
These fins on top of whale sharks help them balance in the water.

tail fin
Also called the caudal fin. Whale sharks sometimes feed with their tails down and mouths pointed up toward the surface.

pectoral fins
Large pectoral fins help sharks steer while swimming.

body
Whale sharks can weigh up to 40,000 pounds (18,144 kilograms). Spot patterns on each whale shark are different.

Picture Glossary

filters
Drains through something.

migrates
Moves to another area at
a particular time of year.

plankton
Tiny animals and plants
that drift or float in oceans
and lakes.

reef
A strip of rock, sand, or coral
close to the surface of the ocean
or another body of water.

Index

To Learn More

Finding more information is as easy as 1, 2, 3.

❶ Go to www.factsurfer.com

❷ Enter "whaleshark" into the search box.

❸ Choose your book to see a list of websites.